THE HURRICURRENT

2011 © Rosamund Stanford
All rights reserved

ISBN: **978-1-928476-54-2**
Deep South
P O Box 6082
Grahamstown 6140 South
Africa
www.deepsouth.co.za

Deep South titles are distributed by
University of KwaZulu-Natal Press
www.ukznpress.co.za

We gratefully acknowledge financial assistance
towards the publication of this book from
Eastern Cape Provincial Arts and Culture Council (ECPACC)
and the National Arts Council (NAC)

Earlier versions of some poems have appeared in
Aerial, New Coin, and sweetmagazine,co.za

Cover art: *'Tree'*, litho print by Willem Boshoff
Text design: Katie Wilter
Cover design: Katie Wilter and Robert Berold

THE HURRICURRENT
Rosamund Stanford

CONTENTS

1 DARK AS DAY
Pa's passing	9
Khehlekazi's hands	10
Dark as day	11
Things we do	12
Daughter-in-lawship	14
Stinkblaar	16
This seeding wind	17
Forefathers	18

2 CLOSE TO THE BONE
Close to the bone	21
Crow sky	22
Far away	25
The colour of teeth	27

3 FLOORDOGS
Glass night	35
Strange heart	36
Like a flying goat	38
Sweep sweep	39
There Robert	40
Floordogs	41
Yes it's warmed up	42
A Wednesday	44

4 MY KNOWING FEELING
Bewell bewell	47
All in my rutted soul	49
My knowing feeling	50
Off the station	51
Standing on end	52
Mind blood	53
All this	54

5 DITCH
Hooves	57
Frame of my mind	58
Lesslessness	59
Ditch	62
Leap day	64
The hurricurrent	66

1: DARK AS DAY

Pa's passing

the time   thinner than the dam starting its ice skin

the soil dark-frozen over our brittle yard
  charcoal frieze of diesel tank and generator,
  chopping block and emptied sacks

nothing stirs the smell of manure or creosote
and the longdrop reeks just faintly through the oaks

we stand   still, like sleeping horses
in awe
before our mourning

Khehlekazi's hands

From that red-brown old ditch
that gets warmer as the day shines out
I see smiling wrinkle-brackets in a dark face
nostrils big as cows'
a whole herd of shiny-shanked Afrikander crossbreds
being lashed into the hissing mist of the race
horns bang and hooves rear,
bewildered faces fight the toxic spray
The disarming atmosphere
of cracking thongs and dung dust
calms me down,
as if I'm sitting in the sneezy msuku grass
watching Khehlekazi's hands
rub dirt out of stiff khakis and
full-square men's handkerchiefs with borderlines
and diminutive lady-handkerchiefs
also having their snot washed off.

Dark as day

trade in the smell of animals
of ox hides twisting with drought
sheep locks thick with grease-coloured lanoline
tight-baled fleeces bound for Durban docks

sump oil draining from the old Nuffield
deep vee-shadows in the rear wheel tread
oblong ruts in the mud of road

the silo casting its tower over the yard
the smoke-choked opening of Bulu's hut
the crevices in his bony old face
throat of an antbear hole

hello little girl in the watergrasses
are you lost in the bliss of day
or have you run away?

Things to do

Putting CMR beetles into tins of paraffin
Holding sheep's jaws open
Opening gates, closing gates
Picking up wire on the road
Pulling jammed logs against the current
to save the bridge's legs
Herding: hens, sheep, cattle, horses
Running with messages:
to the sheep dip, to the engine room,
to the milking shed, to the lovegrass land

Running away from cows,
away from gobbling turkeys,
away from fierce Ncedani
his eyebrows white with mealie dust
Running to catch a horse,
Collecting wet cow dung in buckets,
smearing floors
Moving stones
Pulling out scotch thistles, stinkblaar, and khakibos

Watching: the hammer mill coughing up chaff,
men throwing two-hundred pound mealie
bags onto the trailer,
fingers being stitched back onto hands,
calf hooves emerging out of cowbehinds,
sheep being shorn, sheep being killed,
sheep being skinned,
innards being wiped on the grass,
gall being squeezed onto tripe,
floors being swept, lawns being swept,

lawns being trimmed, lawns being mown,
mealies being felled, the big oak being felled,
Bulu twisting hides into riempies

Waiting: for clouds to move, for rain,
for the fertilizer sales man, for a trip to town,
for Pa to bring marshmallow fish from Williamses.

Daughter-in-lawship

My mother in an apron
with the barber's shears and scissors,
the long silver ones
with a curled bit of metal to protect the finger.

My grandfather on a straight-up chair
a towel over his shoulders
feet squarely on the lawn
socks and brown leather sandals.

'Shouldn't the horses be brought in,
their hooves are getting long
... and that filly'll be getting out of hand
if she isn't handled soon?'

My mother lifts a swathe of hair
from the back of an ear.
Imperceptibly, over the decades his ears have got bigger
or maybe it's his head that's shrunk a bit.

'I'll get her in tomorrow,' says my mother,
clipping the back of the neck.
'She's almost big enough for the long reins,'
says my grandfather.
'She's a very good natured little creature, so
I don't think it matters that we've left things a bit late,'
replies my mother, letting a neat row of hair drop to the grass.

Two hens, proud as illustrations,
go puk-pukking past
pecking invisible things at sudden intervals.

These days my mother leaves the sparsening top strands
a touch longer than before
'His old head feels the cold a bit,' she tells my father
My grandfather cannot see his own crown
and the subtle adaptations she's made to it
in her decades of daughter-in-lawship.

'I'll be having the Seymours out for tea tomorrow,' he says,
'...don't suppose you'd want to join us?'
'Would you like to offer them scones or sandwiches?'
replies my mother.
'You know how Mona loves your brown bread,' says my
grandfather.

She brushes the bits of hair off his neck with the soft baby
brush.
He stands up, shakes his trouser legs, thanks my mother,
walks down the path and under the oaks to his house,
fetches his library book, gives the sky a glance.
My mother goes into our house, fetches a dustpan
sweeps the switches of grey off the lawn.

Stinkblaar

Sinkblaar: lurid and pungent
green-purple skin over
risen-up crests of thorn.

Mad. The pips make you mad as a cow:
a poor beast after an arid earthbound winter.
searching wandering staggering:
big brown mother eyes:
searching for the unseeable greens.

And what is first these days?
These days of camp allotments, fencing off.
Of produce. First are the poison plants.
The ones whose survival equipment is in their sap.
Poor cow: now your nerves are ragwort toxic.

This seeding wind

it billows our shirts and fattens our sleeves
as we lean along trying to hear the tones
of the elderly ones with lucid gazes
the ones who are not closing against this wind
but who look into the slice of each gust
and know it is come to scatter us
and to scatter the trees across lands
so there will be a mix-up
a babel of wattles and willows
sprouting among the mvumvus

Forefathers

Through the neck. On the back
of the back. Bent, bullied, boasted.
Stood. Slept against coir: its lumps.
Bones have stood vertical and held.
Held up. Tall. Hard. Bridges. To the
top of the day. The days. Every day.
Up. Upright. Arrow-browed. Gaunt
bridges: up of the plunging up.
Shouldering bones. Shouldering trees.
Shouldering progeny, storm-sodden
ewes. Raising. Lofted sheds. Planted
poles going high. Roofs lifting to a
pitch. Crops tall as cane. Thatch
streaked by season. Straight and dry.
Trees slowly. All over. Eucalypts. White
shanks into the cloud. Clouds on stalks.
Blood. Litmus of rising days. Sapgreen
insect juices into the up. Up. Standing.
Long cheekbones. Lean. Sculpts. Tall.
Tall hands. Nostril bones. Tall and
aquiline. Foreheads: Forefathers.
Coursing. Coursing. Bone.

2: CLOSE TO THE BONE

Close to the bone

too close to the bone
that's the reason
the reason why
the reason if
the reason that the flatness
it's the reason for the flatness
and for the concentric circles
the unbearably concentric circles
and the pride, the pretending pride
that never relents, never reveals
the crestfallen eye, the crestfallen mouth
the bitter under the stretchedout smile
the held breath of warm flooding loss
the quivering inside the locked jaw
the betrayal in the bones

like this i can't live, like this
yet i do
i can't live so tightly and so sprightly, yet i do
i can't live so roughly and so toughly, but i am
go on, i can't go on, and on and on and on
treading and trodding, all those legs
and legs and legs and legs
and pantyhoses and underpanties
and panting pansies
and prettiness with curvy lipstick
parenthesis of coyness in smiling
and small sanitary fishponds carping with koi
and used-up water filters, clogged
with black stuff like snuff

and used up ozone,
seethrough skyholes
worn out, my favourite soft old shirt
worn through from plain old wear and tear
simple aging

here inside my own house and my own bones
simple shrinking, and bending like an old tree
or a fence pole that's got grey and knotted
and wire uncurling
hair floating to the ground, to the floor
wafting off
wearing out
wear and tear
here and there

Crow sky

on the first year ... a girl ...
they put their heads together
my father and mother... suitable names
good names ... janet
and alice (nothing ostentatious, nothing flamboyant)

and then again
(a year and two months later, March 13 1956)
my mother in the hospital
labouring me
another girl (no debate this time)
let a woman have her fancy
rosamund
rosamund?

like a thief ... 20 years on
there in the farm office
rows and rows of farm diaries
1953 to 1976
I took from the row

Diary 1956
Compliments of East Griqualand Tractors (Pty) Ltd

March 13
(4 items)

2 loads silage
Rosamund born
Hot & fine
4 Fences cut

part of me thought
'it's quite funny'
and again now I think it's quite funny

and some time in between
I was wondering why it was
I'd tried and tried so hard
to follow your eye
into the crow sky

Far away

In China the Earth is square
and the emperor in many respects still 'far away'
It's a comfort knowing there's no point speaking out,
Not even about the unbreathable brown air.

In the windy sleet of winter in a narrow bed
Chen Xiangli sleeps with her coughing granny,
giving us the family's red four-poster heirloom
its feet keeping us above a damp mud floor.

'Are you afraid being in a place of the dead?'
she asks, as we walk back from visiting
her grandfather's waiting tomb:
We see a dead cat strung up in a bush,
'They put it up like that
so it won't stay hidden,'
she explains, quickening her step.

Her own name and her father's name
and her sick grandmother's name
are already engraved on the tombstone.
We saw the characters.

My mother used to buy a tall tin of Tugon poison
with a large grey-black fly on it,
it looked like pink jelly powder.
She hung it all over the place in dangling half tins
with wire handles she'd bent into place
with her strong fingers

Before I went to China I'd pictured Mao killing sparrows
so in the Hangzhou cold I thought China had no wildlife,
even down to flies.
But when summer struck, first there were mosquitoes,
then flies, never a lot of birds though.

There's a fly here now
cleaning its twitchy feelers
I can see the cast of its grey wing-shadows
on a white square of paper
(white in China is the colour of death).

The colour of teeth

Piano keys should be old-teeth white
though I've seen newer pianos with laundry-white notes
I'm sure they lack resonance, ivories must be ivories
Lift the dark lid and the row must be sedately toned
just as the inside of a coconut must be coconut-white
otherwise how do we know if it's sound

A still pool of milk fills about a fifth of a coconut shell
whiter than cows' milk, (although low fat
or no-fat milk has a bluish tinge)
the knife slips easily when I slice shapes
from the cracked-open hardness of coconut

Tubey vein-hoses make a wiggly fan
across the back of my hand
my skin must be transparent
because the vein-blue blue is visible through it
This is my return piping, and my blue blood
now teeming with vanquished pathogens,
is flowing, in the main, against the gravity
that draws my watery being down
as inexorably as my molars erode chew by chew

In America they clip off the points of hens' beaks
so they can't tear each other to pieces
in the drawers where they are fattening in layers
They also give milk-cows false teeth
so the whole beast lasts longer (bovine orthodontia)

We humans are okay:
to survive, we don't have to have teeth,

because of chewless foodstuffs,
Like hydroponic plants, we can exist for decades
on drips through tubes
Our teeth can be reserved for smiles – job interviews
mood-transmission and luring mates for dates
Our rows must be gleamy-white, no gaps
and no overlaps
And if you rub your teeth with charcoal
although it's very black and gritty
they become more smooth and white
That's what Sarah showed me
She used to wash our wash with washing blue
It was the size of a block of yeast
but a deep early-evening blue that made sheets white

I used to want to be in an advertisement
bright clothes and bright teeth
But despite all my trudges down Hope Street
with Sister Loyola gripping my arm
(even though I knew perfectly well
if a car was coming) and opening my jaws
in Dr Theron's pump-up chair
my left front incisor still slightly overlaps
the right one
I haven't got a perfect smile

It's hard to see a horse's teeth
So if you feed a horse something
like half an apple, with one of your hands
you are liable to think its herbivorous
velvety-black horse lips can do you no harm
My sister Janet thought that: she offered a horse
half her golden delicious, in a clutching hand

Watching, it appeared quite delicate to me
as if the horse's lips just sucked
her thumbskin and nail right off
But it was really his huge hidden off-white
horse-teeth that scraped her thumb clean

The other day a mare was sniffing at the fig tree
as we rode past
so I got off, picked a fig
then flattened my hand out like a plate
with the fig perched on it
She wrenched it with her camel mouth
and chewed with the thick iron bit across her tongue
Worse than braces I imagine, even so
she wanted more and more figs
I picked overripe ones, small flies
buzzing around their gum-pink openings,
you never know with figs if the villi-like fingers
will start wriggling or not
but horses are not squeamish

I don't eat horsemeat, although
I'm quite ashamed of the fact that I eat other animals
and recently I seem to have become more
rather than less carnivorous.
although I ate spinach for breakfast
It's my latest fetish

It's taken me decades to like spinach
It always tasted bitter and looked like sloppy cow dung
when cooked by the cook-nun at the Kokstad Convent
I suppose cooking for large numbers isn't inspiring
specially the three-sit-down-meals-a-day treadmill

When I was a kid breakfast was a formal meal
First yellow mealie-meal porridge (if it was winter)
and puthu if it was summer
with amaas, sugar and cream
As we moderned up a bit we got breakfast cereal as well
No one would have dreamt of having just cereal though
We'd sprinkle a few sparse flakes like fallen leaves
on top of the porridge

The milk had a thick hem of cream and
there was always a jug of cream on the table too
The cream came out of the thin spout of the separator
yellower, with wrinklier wrinkles than the milk
which flowed in a loose spiral out of the fatter spout
The milking shed smelled of cows' breath, salt, sheep locks,
and sometimes the vomity smell
of not properly washed milking muslins

In a magazine yesterday, I think it was a New Yorker
they had a review of a European art exhibition
A whole range of milking stools,
most of them variations on the toadstool
some in pastel plastics
One with a baby milking stool on a side stalk
(maybe for the udder-grease pot)
The milkers on our farm used to sit
on dark greasy tree-stumps
And if a cow was a kicker, like unruly Nozinja,
whose name meant something like 'the one of the dogs'
then she'd get her legs tied up with twisted riempies
before getting her finger-pink teats wiped, greased and
nearly all the milk squeezed out

Turnips were one of the things that cows ate
which made the milk smell completely disgusting
There was a special thing, like an iron walking stick,
with blades in a cross shape, that was used
to chop up turnips so that they wouldn't
stick in cows' throats like a tennis ball

I wasn't mad about the smell of milk in the first place
and when it stank of turnip breath I had to
block my nose before I could eat my porridge.
That's how I discovered that most of my taste buds
are actually in my nose, which was lucky for me
It meant that even though the liver
cooked by the cook nun was frighteningly repulsive
and even though I would have got into trouble
if I'd pinched my nostrils shut in the refectory
I found I was able to lift the back of my tongue
so it blocked off the airholes between my mouth and nose
Then I couldn't taste the unspeakable smell
and I didn't have to get punished for not being able to eat
a moss-green piece of liver, with cut-off vein tubes

3: FLOORDOGS

Glass night

I have a beautiful heirloom
sparkly-severed angles
small enough to hold a small egg
on a thin leg
not scrawny like a hen's leg
elegant   a pedestal
casting a cut-grey shape across
the lines of the oregon cleared table

the liquor is still
I poured it not to drink
but as a companion
so I could view the glass
in its distilled fullness

so I could have a smoking partner
so I could put on my best
meet myself in style
and sip cold dry paleness on a night
when out there
the sky and all its people, all its sparks
are too far away to feel

Strange heart

I've met you in your handsomeness
your arms, attached squarely to your shoulders
your chest, a standing shield
your belly, full as a commanding chief's

I've met the boy
right pupil pi r squared
hands limp

I try
to navigate your big head dome
your lynx ear feathers
to round your manbody

gently (without violence) you lift my fingers
replace my hands   back on my own arms
and I stand   millimetres from your breath
cast
like lot's wife in some form of pinioned
pillar although unlike
(whatever her name)
my disobedience lies
in looking forward
following my hands
touching

so   despite myself,
despite me trying   and succeeding somewhat
to hold my
chest out, my buttocks in
and my chin high,

    my warm
like wee trickling down the thighs
of a child unheld
is seeping away

Like a flying goat

like a flying goat
limbed legs hanging
a wasp comes down
settles against the pane

it sees green through the glass
that doesn't open
feelers swim the window
then it tips its head back
and we look up together at sky

I try to not go too far with clouds
but today there's a dog,
only its snout-tip sooted
it has a forked tail

to my left
there's a rust-coloured door ajar
and half a wagon wheel
spoked finely
like sliced citrus

the wasp is doubling its knees
against the slidy hardness

i snatch at a wingtip
dodging its thistle-thin syringe
then fling its body
into the billiard-green air

Sweep sweep

Daily I sweep sweep
sweep the greyblack floor
Big pool of floor
Sweep
Bits of earth, crisp grass wisps,
cat hairs, crumbs, a curve of onion
Sweep

What has happened to our weather?
Everyone is cold.
But the grasses are rampaging.
Swishing about in phalanxes.
Covering the land.
Long foresting shafts.
Growing, growing, growing.

And this summer it rains
and stays cool
and gets colder
Day after day after day

There Robert

You stonish toadish thing
camouflaged in your cave
of crumbling grimy walls
birds on the outside,
loudly stab stab stabbing
at the murky panes

Floordogs

the evening, filled with breathable drops
and we, the two of us
in this lone partnership on this veering craft
helmless, stone-walled
at least now there's a veil,
softening us and the bathwater,
you first then me, soaping myself in your aftermath,
opening our pores, shaking off the drops
and we are almost, almost able to look about
the way dogs who know each other simply look
here's a dog, there's another one scratching its belly
with a hind paw, lying on the floor, getting up
to be nearer to another dog, also lying on the floor

Yes it's warmed up

Luckily there were poppies full of lantern light
and upturned smiles
So for a moment she forgot the hollow
for she had a large hollow;
And all around, up went mountains, as sheer and sudden
as any to be seen in a Chinese watercolour
The poppies were not only light,
they gave back the orange of an orange,
but more luminous
burning through their parasol petals.
They were anything but orange, she was thinking
with a slight sense of disillusionment.
And their legs were hairy:
her own legs had ten minutes earlier been hairy;
but what had she done?
A sneaky thing:
Even husbands don't like their razors borrowed for legs,
so what a cheek to use her ex's razor.
Yet undeterred she'd shaved her calves smooth:
it was one of those ones with three rows of blades,
very efficient.
Her leg bristles by now were way down into the sewers
under Johannesburg;
And where was her lover?
He was elsewhere, in fact he'd gone to China.
It was from him that she had hoped for an email:
What would she have liked him to say in it?
Dear Rosamindy, that was a name she liked him to use:
and she would hear him then with his gentle voice
saying her name: and her belly would soften.

She would have liked to feel his hands moulding her sides,
so she said: I'll stand quite still and all I will do
is feel your hands going wherever they go.
His fingers in her eyes had become gently green and soft.
She could see the grain of his hands
as beautiful as wood in its lines, but much finer than wood;
His arms were long as lovely planks:
undulating planks all the way from China.
They were supple, and the wood grain flowed.
She felt the carving of her sides:
and then he said: I think your breasts are far away.
And she said yes: they are here on this fat continent,
listening for the weather: when it warms they soften
and when it colds they tighten: they have been alone
for so long; and now they are alert with cold.
With his eyes he saw her breasts:
and then she could hear him speak
all the way from a high-up clifflike wedge
of Chinese mountain:
I shouldn't have let them be cold for so long;
I should have put my warm mouth over first this one
then that one, I should have warmed your breasts.
Yes, she said, you should have warmed them.

A Wednesday

here under this pinsome rain
trees dripping their flappy ears
and my two pinnae, neat next to my sideskull
curled cartilages growing on my head
two listening holes to navigate me
head tilted a bit: rain, millions of it,
roof of rain over my haired head
pouring into my listening ear
wet-grass air in the noseholes
chink of spoon on a cup
a man making toast
under the rain roof

4: MY KNOWING FEELING

Bewell bewell

slip and your left leg'll part company
with your right, it'll drop simply
like a birch log through an icehole
to the slimy silty bottom, and your right leg
still joined at the hip to your ropey neck
will be dragged by your hard-pupilled eyes
across speedlimitless autobahn after autobahn
to the upholstery of conferences, pre-prepared scripts
earphone interlocution
water vases with reintroduced minerals
inputs:outcomes
reciprocity and ingredient-swapping
the politeness of intellectual private properties
titles in deed

the salve of precooked decisions
we can return our quicks neatly to the allotted slot
on each finger tip
fix the crucifixion for friday
we own the rights too
tippex out dissenting blemishes: shine, shine, clip our lips
thirty silver pieces a second
allow the air-conditioning to re-inflate our alveoli
with wrung-out air from inside walls
yes yes yes we agree

your right hand will be shaking then wiping off the terms
touching escalators then wiping off the germs
your clothes will be worn once and incinerated
your money spent once then laundered
your shit will be shat into cleanly chlorinated water

then flushed
your dogs fed pellets from high-resolution labels
your children will be fed wordsallgluedtogether
unusable except in gaudy clauses for pre-stated causes

your eyes and your children's eyes
will be fastforwarded and rewound and fast forwarded
and rewoundandfastforwarded and rewounded
and the hard drive of your eyes will get its gazy glaze again
and your chin will be ajutting and you will be astrutting
and all will be wrapped up, flushing and flashing
and nobody will cast asides and spread remarks
emails will confine themselves
to the business of busyness
and you will be well
bewell bewell
and bewell
and all will be well

All in my rutted soul

I hear a thief calling:
I'm here to smooth your way
to let you lie and rest
I'm carrying your buckets
of tar. Black, sticky, foetid, full.
You may see a smile, even a grin.
But this. This wide opening
is simply the shape of my mouth
And these oblongs
are the shape of my eyes.
I go back you see. Back.
I am the what of back.
I am the thief of you.

My knowing feeling

my knowing feeling has left
with its rigid and sullen moustache
it sat staring along shelves
thick black lines lined up
and slits of skin showing between.
I'm glad it's out of me:
like a man with too many daughters
and a hoping wife,
the trouser legs of my knowing feeling
were too big for its legs.

Off the station

All along
it's the song, making itself,
trying to make itself heard
All along it's been there, but no
I will not hear it
It's playing
all the time it's playing
it's here
But no I will not hear.
I can even say, to myself: I want to die
But I will not hear
I can say: yes I want to die
But no I will not hear it
There: no not there: here
Yes here
It is here
I want to die
That's what I hear
But who is saying it?
Myself: with my lips
Moving like rubbery waves
What? What: they are saying: What?
As if they are the ears
My wavy lips have become my ears
Speaking and listening
They are seething with sound
Out of tune, off the station
My ears are deafening me
And my mouth is slowly trying
its odd undulations
A lonely speaking mouth
moving in silence.

Standing on end

Me with my matching clothes
the adipose padded matron
So much lead in my cells
giving me this thickened head
My eyes look out, bulge
My olfactory receptors: fumigated into retraction
My hive, seething with notes of refinement
The beautiful language is lacquering over
and the porous and gracious bones
are standing on end

Mind blood

this courtroom convincing
I'm in the habit of
makes me mistrust my own waters
I have the arguments
about everything,
about toughing it through
the length or strength of blood,
but my veins
seamy in the end
are giving me away
letting some of it out
of the bloodsome mud

All this

I will have to stand here
I will have to live my biliousness
Till molecule by molecule it has effused me
Till molecule by molecule it has left my liver
Every particle every hue
I will have to feel the grains
Through the sieve of my self
I will have to sweat and lie down
I will have to run and wring myself out
I will have to unclench my cheeks
I will have to soften my gaze
I will have to relax my wrung out neck
I will have to do all this
before there is quiet for me

5: DITCH

Hooves

No one is here
in this pit of a grey-ribbed valley
hulk of a stony ark

I watch the sound of a far up train
judder through the walls
and the floorboards' hollow shiver

I've waited so long down here
hunkered like a frog when hooves pass
in the night of night

Frame of my mind

you. yes you. wooden iron construct. eye-box
earbox, breath regulator, bank vault, spirit level
I break my shoulder — my horizontal collar
just to get me out of this over-aged, oversized scaffold
I will. yes I will. infirm your firmity

Lessnessness

I'm grateful like a Christian
for the bumps of earth
under my slippers
  the sheep I'm stood up on
  laid its skin down
  and its locks
  to be footpadding
  felting of ground
  softed

and through them
the bumps
telling me
  lower
  it's lower
  the pace

  the pace is lower

  walk on my ears
the bumps
the bumps are telling me

  still
  be still
  in the heave and hive
  still
  as the queen   laying

  crawl the slow-roll bank
  feel

feel the matted matting
of end-of-winter bits
broken-off msuku grass
dust-silted

roll   till a stone
or a rock
heaves up
under my shoulder blade

and through the valley
the wind
from its rushing tear
stops   all of a sudden

Ditch

So I tried, tried living in a ditch
couldn't hear the acoustics down there
and the smell was grainy
my drums loosened a bit, got softer and quiet,
I was quiet and quietened, talkless, and when I talked
it came out loud, words strode forth
No, I thought, turn them round, bend them over
put them back, cocoon them

I kept some fat between my bones and my skin,
for cushioning purposes.
It was a good thing, I could lie quite still
and the cold came, but only slowly,
and quite quietly.
At first I'd felt warm,
warm as another person's warm shirt
warm as a streaming blonde day
Then the sun dropped over the edge,
risen out of my ditch, moved on.

That's okay I said, okay for it to vanish.
But I was not convinced.
It was propaganda of the kind kind,
the sort that mothers and their soothy ilk
had bathed me in:
No such thing as gloom, not in our life,
our life is very merry.

I lay there thinking of my formerly tight mouths
and cleanliness and warmliness and Stuttafords bra section
and my two breasts and how my shoulders cowed

forward to shelter them.
In the ditch my breasts were fine,
round and braless, they were lying quiet, silently and lazily,
one atop my chest, the other bulging a bit
over the edge of me.

They didn't mind anymore, of which I was glad.
They were comfortable for a change
even though it was extremely uncomfortable were I was.
In fact I would have liked a mattress,
but mattresses spring out of their seams in ditches,
show their skeletons. In any case
it's illogical to think you can have a mattress in a ditch
and I had logic on my side.

I had enough unseemly fat to cushion the earth
which, as I soon found out, was quite grateful
for the consideration I was showing it.
It: I thought. Is that alright:
a right way to think of the earth?
But what else is there: I've never been
one to think of the earth as a she
or cars either, and specially not ships (maiden voyages),
there's something obscene in calling a vessel she
(or the other way round).

It was uncomfortable as the night bore on
Not that I'd been expecting sleep,
I was awaiting and awaking, but parts of me
my eyes for example, were adroop,
I was like a hen or a horse, standing and sleeping
(although I wasn't sleeping and neither was I standing,
but I could just as well have been

for all the comfort of lying on that lumpen earth).
I didn't wish to be rude to the earth,
either the bits of it that I was lying on
or the whole thing
I was less comfortable than even those people
who used a stool-like carved thing for a pillow,
(rows and rows of them are on display in Museum Afrika).
Maybe they were better than a rock,
and good at stopping insects crawling into your earhole
and for keeping the earth-sound out.

I could hear the earth,
it was embarrassing, it was breathing,
but not in a relaxed continental way, not easy earthbreath.
It was breathing as if it knew someone had
their ear right on it, it couldn't completely let go.
If the sun had been shining it probably wouldn't
have minded my ear following each in and each out,
but at night with everything so quietened
the earth didn't feel free.
I began to feel intrusive: 'I'll not hear' I said,
and for a while the earth breathing did ease a bit,
began to sound like the far-off swishing sea
but soon enough it realised that my ear was actually
not blockable, that my breathing was the breathing
of pretending to not listen, or not to hear,
that I couldn't not hear. So I gave up trying to not listen
and both of us, me and the earth, softened a bit.

Leap day

it was the day before leap day
of the year two thousand
divisible by four
a lucky year all in all

the long-transplanted deodars
dirtier than bottle green
were laying down spires of shadow
and an old gramophone arm
lofted into place
was already spinning a voice
between revolving lanes
passing under the needle

my conscience had slidden
out of commandment
the slab worn soft:
a weathered dishcloth
fit for a cheek.
the faces had got older and younger
the eyes deeper

a fine warmish rasp
the tongue of a cat
licked my joints

there were many things:
skirts held up from the dew
of the diamond-cold lawn

morning already lit
by the fearsome sun
of the new century

The hurricurrent

from the mess of stalks and twigs
a stirring was stirring,
shaping me inside my hard parts
my tail moving about,
my sticking-about legs and mind bones
in an iron-filing hurri-current
an untidying soundless tide

www.ingramcontent.com/pod-product-compliance
Lightning Source LLC
Chambersburg PA
CBHW070334180426
43196CB00050B/2679